A PURPOSE AND A HELPER

By

Ugochi B. Akinmoladun

God has a purpose for everyone He created

He created you and I for a purpose.

Do not underestimate yourself, you are a helper.

Table of Contents

Dedication

This book is dedicated to the Almighty God, who is the source of my inspiration. He sowed the seed of knowledge in my mind and nourished it. His wisdom is beyond human imaginations. I am forever grateful to God. All glory belongs to Him.

Acknowledgement

I could not have embarked on this journey without the help of God. I am eternally grateful to Him for the grace He has bestowed on me to understand His revealing love. I would like to appreciate my parents and siblings for their great love and prayers, especially my late father, Sunday Umere, for his words of encouragement that fill my heart each and everyday. I would like to appreciate all the members of RCCG Restoration Villa, Queens, New York, and Dover Assembly, Delaware, for their unwavering support, and prayers. My deepest appreciation goes to my wonderful children for their great understanding, encouragement, support, and motivation.I would like to express my sincere gratitude to my Sweetheart, and destiny helper, Dr. Francis Akinmoladun for his unconditional love and mentorship. He inspires me in various ways. I would love to extend my appreciation to Emma Felix, and Robert MIlls for their constant support and motivation. I wish to extend my special thanks to everyone who has provided me with helpful resources toward the progress of this book. This effort would not have been accomplished without your love and support.

To everyone reading this book today, I would like to say thank you for being part of this great success. May God richly bless you

About the Author

Ugochi B. Akinmoladun is the author of "A Crown of Glory," an assistant Pastor at The Redeemed Christian Church of God, Restoration Villa. She is passionate about helping people through her unique gifts from God. She likes reading, writing, and traveling. She holds an Associate Degree, in Liberal Art, and Sciences in Queensborough Community College, New York, a Bachelor's Degree in Psychology in Queens College, and presently, a graduate student study for a MSW at Delaware State University. She is happily married to Pastor, Dr. Francis Akinmoladun and blessed with five wonderful children.

INTRODUCTION

The journey of life is full of memories, challenges, surprises, celebrations, highs and low that impact our lives. We all need someone to help us irrespective of their religion or social status. This has been the nature of life since the beginning of man. God made a man and realized that man could not be alone without a helper so He made woman that would help the man to fulfil destiny. (Genesis 2:18). God is the greatest helper of all. He is the source of our help. In fact, our help comes from Him, the Holy One that created the Heavens and earth. We enjoy His Supernatural help daily. We cannot do without Him. However, He has assigned people to help each person to fulfilling divine mandate. There are people He has empowered, and equipped specifically for you to help you get to your maximum potential in life. He uses men to help men through life's obstacles and pleasant results. Whatever you do, you need someone to help you accomplish your goals. For instance, a farmer who has acres of land with palm trees needs a producing company for production before it gets to the consumers for consumption. All this will come to realization with the help of men that God has blessed with different steps of plantation agriculture in order to help the farmer. The farmer cannot do it all alone. In other words, we all need someone to help us reach our goals in life irrespective of who they are. There is an adage that says " a single tree does not make a forest". This means that no one can adequately build a city without the support of others. This book, "A Purpose and a Helper", differentiates and explains in details three types of Destiny helpers. You will get to know who are destiny helpers, what are their motives, and how to identify them. As you read this book today, the Lord will direct your helpers to you at every point in your life in Jesus's name. Amen!

CHAPTER ONE
Destiny Helper

Who are destiny helpers? Or Have you helped someone or you were helped by somebody before? Destiny helpers are the people God has prepared and ordained to help you achieve your divine purpose. As a matter of fact, we are created to help each other. God is the only one who can help people to help others. He has made provisions for everyone to be helped one way or the other. He has prepared somebody for you and I so you are not alone in this world. In the book of Psalms 121:1-2, it reads, " I lift up my eyes from the hills, from where does my help come? My help comes from the Lord, who made Heaven and earth". Our divine help comes from God, He can use anyone as your helper to connect, assist, support, lift, encourage, and endorse you. It could be a lay man, so do not underestimate anyone you encounter in life, because sometimes, God uses ordinary people to perform the extraordinary. There are different kinds of people with different mindsets that are placed to accompany an individual fulfill divine destiny. There are people you meet for the first time and your life will change for the best, these are people that are there to help you no matter how life has been. The ability to accommodate and celebrate people that you come across in your life is important. The story of Mordecai in the book of Ester chapter 2, is a relevant example of someone who is assigned to help Ester.

In addition, Ester has been with Mordecai after her parents died. Technically, he was her guardian, and had been supporting, protecting, and providing for all her needs and stood as a father figure for her. He raised her up from a younger age to adult. Mordecai took her as his own child making sure her spiritual, emotional, and psychological needs are met. He did not let her feel the loss of her parents by bridging the gap. He was her mentor and encourager. He was the one that handed her over to Hegai, the king's eunuch who is in charge of the women, that an audition for a new queen. At the end of the audition, Ester found favor in the sight of the king and eventually became the queen. God puts Mordecai into Ester's life to help her fulfill her purpose of delivering the people of Isreal. If her parents were still alive, there was a probability that Ester would not be the queen at that time, but Mordecai was the actual person who God assigned to assist her to become who she was created to be. He was a destiny helper to Ester. Destiny helpers are sent from God to help you fulfill your destiny in life.

This is related to our time today, that someone, somewhere has been created to be the head of an establishment but needs someone to connect you to that person that has been divinely assigned for you. Someone is responsible for your lifting, promotion, and breakthrough. Be appreciative when you find your helper.

Furthermore, I remembered some years ago as a teenager, I was dropped out from High School because my parents could not afford to pay for my school fees. On this fateful day, I was alone in my room thinking about what my future would look like without an education. In that hopeless and helpless situation, I cried and prayed for a couple of hours not knowing that God was preparing a greater and glorious days ahead of me. The next day, I was convinced to leave where I was staying to another city and I did. Even though I did not understand what was going on but I knew God was with me. On the Sunday, I went to a church very close to where I stay and the first person that greeted me happened to be my destiny helper who help changed my life today. In fact, we are best friends. By God's grace, we are happily married with wonderful children. Every little thing, he did for me, I always show a profound appreciation and respectful, not knowing he was paying attention to my gesture. Be careful how you treat people around you, everyone you meet in life has something to offer, pay attention and learn from them, they are contributing to your lifting, they are there for a purpose. Some are there for a short time, while others are there for a long period of time. Whenever their time might be, do not take them for granted, God brought them to your life for a significant reason. I have come across many people who had treated people unfair in the past and needed their help at some point. Life is unpredictable, you cannot tell what will happen in the next second, so value everyone you encounter in this journey of life, because we all have what it takes to help each other. Do not look down on anyone, because everyone is specially created to offer something. Treat the maids you keep in your house with respect, they are your destiny helpers. They are there rendering services that you are unable to render to yourself, so treat them well.

Additionally, everyone has the potentials to be a destiny helper, as you are reading this today, you are somebody's destiny helper. Reflect on your life and think of how you can help others because you have been helped by someone in the past or right now. You arc not where you are today without being helped by somebody you know or not. Your life is governed by God, He arranges and brings strangers you never met to help you. He does whatever He wants to do because He is our Divine Destiny Helper. Always remember to appreciate your creator who divinely placed relevant people to your path to help your destiny because without Him you are nobody. He brought them to help you accomplish a goal, so you are expected to be a helper to someone else. Change your world by helping others fulfilling their destinies. Luke 12 : 17 says, Jesus said I have come to fulfill what that has been written. WHAT HAVE YOU COME TO FULFILL?

5

CHAPTER TWO
Destiny Pusher

Are you being discouraged by how things are not working out the way you expected? Do not be discouraged when things are not going the way you planned, everything works for a reason. The Almighty God is a great and perfect planner. He allows certain things to come your way for you to be stronger and wiser. Even in the darkest moment of your life, when you think the world is against you, He is always with you. Do not belittle the presence of God in your life, His plans for you may not be known by your limited understanding. But He is arranging things in sequence for your good. Nothing happens for nothing, everything that happens to a person has a purpose for its occurrence. In the book of Romans 8:28, it states, " And we know that all things work together for good, to them that love God, to them who are the called, according to His purpose" So, do not panic, trust God in the midst of trials and temptations. Praise and adore Him more. He delays somethings to make things happen. He is the only one that can go back to the past and correct the mistakes we had made. He knows the beginning to the ending, and from the ending to the beginning, because He lives in the past, present, and future. He controls the affairs of all men, and orders their footsteps. His understanding is far beyond the imaginations of human beings. I marvel how God listens and attends to more than 8 billion people in the world at the same time, what a marvelous God. He knows every challenge you face daily. He brings people into your life for a reason you may not comprehend at the moment until it manifests. So, do not look down on anyone you come across in life.

In addition, God uses people to push people forward in order to fulfill their mission in life. Joseph was a perfect example of a man who experienced a push from his brothers. His brothers pushed him to his destiny. His push came at the right time, if not for his brothers, he would not get to fulfill his purpose as a prime minister. His brothers were his destiny helpers in disguise. It has been planned out that his own blood brothers were the ones that would sell him out to get to where his destiny would manifest. They saw themselves as failures and slaves to their brother after he narrated his dreams to them. They did not see beyond the dream. This is the All-Knowing God at work. He makes things happen in His own way. Nobody can understand how He works. When Joseph was appointed as the Prime Minister, he remembered his family, same people who sold him out to strangers. He invited them to come, He literally forgave them because he knew it was God's plans for his life. Gen. 45: 5-8 NIV. This indicated that God was the one behind the scene. He erased the hatred of his brothers from his memory. Genesis chapter 37, the story of how Joseph was sold to strangers was narrated. The brothers planned to kill him but one of them said they should throw him in the pit and later sold him out. They thought he was going to die anyway, not knowing that God used them to fasten what had been revealed in the past. Joseph had to go through tough times before his dreams manifested. It was part of God's plans for him. God has orchestrated our journey on earth. The scripts of the journey of our lives are in His hands. Each person has a script that is different from others. Everyone needs to identify his or her script to be able to work according to the script so he or she does not act as someone else. Every script is involved with people who are meant to push you to your destiny. God knows how to make things happen at the right time. He knew it was the right time to push Joseph into the pit to be able to be seen by the Ishmaelites that would continue the process of his journey to destiny. During the process to his destiny, God never left him by himself, He was with him through the journey. When family and friends betray you, and when people you love so dearly disappoint you, do not take it personal, do not see them as your enemies, instead change your perspective regarding the situation. It is a time to reflect and seek God's will concerning your destiny. Pray more, express your gratitude to God, learn from the experience, and love them more. This is because for every disappointment, there is a greater blessing. There are people who God has purposely placed to push you forward, if not, you will not make a move, so, appreciate them when you encounter them. It is part of your destiny that you will go through challenges, and disappointments before you move forward. Your testimony is not complete without the experience. They are people who make great impact in your life. You may perceive it as a negative influence, but it has to be. They are your destiny pusher. If people who caused you pain were not there, you would not have taken a step forward, you would not get to where you are today. You need them to grow spiritually, psychologically, materially, and financially. You must pass all your prerequisites before your light begins to shine. Everyone has a different experience, no need to complain, you are coming out of it stronger and cleaver. God is with you always.

Joseph passed all his examinations before he became the prime minister. Even when he was in the prison, he did not blame his brothers for their hatred and immaturity. In fact, it was not recorded that he mentioned it to the people around how he got to the strange land. He did not compare his destiny to others because he knew where God was taking him to. He did not lose focus of his mission. He always remembered what he saw in his dreams, and that gave him more assurance about his destiny. He focused on God's revelations of him. He relayed on His Word concerning him. He was obedient, respectful, disciplined, and courageous. These attributes helped him overcome life's challenges. 1 Peter: 3: 9, states, "Do not repay evil with evil or insult with insult. On the contrary, repay evil with blessing, because to this you are were called so that you may inherit a blessing". This means that, no matter the evil people did to you or doing to you now, do not revenge. Do not fight back or blame them. Never compare yourself to others because your destiny is different. You are original not a photocopy. Regardless of where you are or what you are going through right now because of someone's else mistakes, do not revenge. However, pray for them, bless them that cause you pain, for your blessings to overflow. God is a God of principles, He will ask you to do something for you to gain more. Some people keep records of wrongs, and disappointments in their lives. This will not let you see the plans of God for your life. Others are distracted by complaining and blaming others for their situations and some compare their present condition to others. Everyone is going through one issue or the other. No need for comparison. In any condition you find yourself, give thanks to God because He knows about it, He sees beyond what you are going through now. So, if you are being pushed by people around you, take it as a reminder to move forward. Embrace the push, learn from the push, grow from the push, and focus on your mission to fulfilling your destiny. The Almighty God will crown each step you take forward with success.

CHAPTER THREE
Destiny Connector

Destiny connectors are the people God has predestined to connect you to the people who have the ability to positively influence your life. God works through people to achieve His purpose no matter their age, He can use anyone. The original assignment of a connector is to connect you to people who God has ordained for you. These are the people who are willing to sacrifice themselves for others to succeed in life. They believe in God's assignment for their lives. They want to see you succeed no matter what. They see what you cannot you see in your life. They see the light and glory of God in you, so they encourage every step you take to moving forward. Destiny connectors are people who stand in between you and your helper. The introduction, recommendation, and information you need to fulfill your destiny are in people. In the case of Naaman, it was the little maid that got the information of a prophet who God had been using to perform miracles and advised Namaan's wife to inform him, as a result, he was healed from leprosy. (2 Kings 5:2-3) So, your destiny needs a connector to connect you to them. They might not have the resources you need at a time, but they know people who are capable to lift you up above limitations of life. They are ordained by God to get you to your purpose in life.

In other words, there are uncountable forces that are working tirelessly to stop you from achieving your purpose in destiny. John 10:10 states that "The thief comes only to steal and kill and destroy; I have come that they may have life, and have it to the full" It means that the devil wanders around to abort destinies, he delights in destroying talents. A lot of intelligent people with great potentials have died uncelebrated because no one discovered them. To be able to fight against these forces, you need to know the Word of God concerning you, the knowledge of who you are, and discerning spirit that will help you identify people who are divinely connected to your destiny. The Will of God concerning you is to give you a healthy and satisfying life, this is the reason He made adequate provision for you. You need a destiny connector at every point of your journey to destiny. As you journeying through life to destiny be aware of the kind of people you meet on the way. Everyone is not going to where you are going, be watchful and prayerful. Many people have missed their destiny connectors because of pride, and ignorance, so they broke the relationship. Some look down on them because they believe they are not in position to help. Sometimes, Destiny connectors do not look as they are. They could be your friends, colleagues, teachers, family members, and strangers. It is not about their physical appearance but about who is leading them to you. Do not disconnect your connection with your destiny connector. Be patient, be determined, be positive and consistent in everything you do. Your Destiny connector will locate at the right time.

MY PURPOSE

I had no choice where and when I would be born on earth, but Almighty God brought me from eternity into eternity and redesigned me for His glory. I am immensely grateful to Him for His unquestionable sacrifice for me and family. Before the beginning of everything, He has been existing, His Kingdom is everlasting.

CHAPTER ONE
I know You

Every living creature is created by the only One who has being before the beginning of times and will be forever. He was God yesterday, He is God today, and will always be God. He created times and made times out of times to form human, so he knows everything about you. The Scripture made it clear that "Before I formed you in the womb I knew you, and before you were born I consecrated you; I appointed you a prophet to the Nations." (Jeremiah 1:5) God knows you more than you know yourself, even before your parents come together. No one has the power to create his or herself. He is the only one that has the power to create and recreate things. He has your life in His hands so you are not a stranger to Him. He knows your name before you were given the name. He made you what He wants you to be in life. He has deposited power, talent, wealth, strength, wisdom, health, and knowledge in you to use according to His plans for you. He has given you everything that you need to fulfill your purpose in life, because He chose you before you were born. He has ordained and blessed you from your mother's womb. Your mission on earth has be prepared before the existence of time, so whatever you are is the manifestation of a finished work of the Almighty God for your life.

The journey of every life is being monitored by the owner of the life. Every living creature has a purpose to fulfil within a period of time. In fact, Times and seasons have a target to meet so they don't waste opportunities. You are made to fulfil the reason why you are created. Everyone is formed with a significant purpose and assignment to be completed. He brought you to this world to show forth His glory to the World. This means that Everyone carries the glory of God, no one is created without a glory. The time of manifestation of glories is different. The glory must be manifested for the whole world to see and praise the creator of all glories. The purpose of God in your life must be fulfilled, irrespective of challenges you face. He never allowed you to walk alone. He is always with you to guide you toward your purpose in life. Jeremiah 29:11 says, " For I know the thoughts that I think toward you, declares the Lord, thoughts of peace and not evil, to give you a future and a hope" He assures you in His words about his plans for you on earth, that He will not let you go astray, He will not let you down, He will not betray you, and will always lead you to the right directions. He has everything concerning everyone worked out in His calendar, and His will is to help everyone through the journey of life with ease because He has their life in His hands. He watches and leads you to where He wants you to go. There is nothing that happens to you that He is not aware of, He knows and sees everything. No one can hide from God, His eyes are opened to the ways of all creatures. What you do every second is being recorded by the owner of time. He is the only one that knows the beginning to the ending of the people He created. Whatever you acquire on earth is from God. He releases to you so you can make use of it to accomplish your purpose. Everyone is given according to their strength, God has given each and everyone's gifts to utilize according to their abilities. The expectation is to walk according to His purpose for your life and not deviate from it. Each person is allocated with different assignments for a particular purpose. I have come to realize that everyone has a reason to be alive and we all have different times of existence. Our life spans are not the same. So, if you are reading this right now, that means you are a living being with a divine purpose. Your life is determined and controlled by the one who knows you more than you know yourself, in fact, your parents do not know you more than your creator. There is nothing you do without him knowing about it. He allows whatever pleases Him to happen to you so lean on Him to journey through life with you. He knows the beginning, middle, and ending of time. He has been existing before He decided to create you and I.

CHAPTER TWO
Who are You

The recognition of one's capacity to develop certain characteristics as an individual in the future is self-identification. A lot of factors contribute in building who you are as a person. However, you are created with a unique personality. There is a great you inside of you that only the power given to you from God can unveil it. There is a spirit that is working inside of you to help make you what you are. Often times, the environment where people grow up contribute in building up the kind of person they are but not the You. People that you come across have influence in you and places you live or go to also contribute to your growth, but not You. Many factors help shape people's characters in life, but most importantly is knowing what you are created to be. Identifying your abilities and disabilities is the beginning of knowing who you are and why you are here. There is a great power you carry that is not transferrable. You must be able to identify the effect of the power inside of you. For instance, asking yourself reflection questions, like, who am I? Why am I here? What is my purpose? And where am I going? A regular assessment of self is very important in life, it keeps you focused. Also, understanding who you are is the key to fulfilling a purpose. In 1 Perter 2:9, it states, "But you are a chosen generation, a royal priesthood, a holy nation, His own special people, that you may proclaim the praises of Him who called you out of darkness into His marvelous light" The knowledge that you have been chosen by the Supreme God before the beginning of time is enough conviction that you are a special creature with a unique purpose.

In addition, indentifying your identity in God is understanding the meaning of life. Understanding the meaning of life, is the beginning of self-realization. You are a chosen person, you are different from others, you carry a unique personality, a potential that no one else carries, your uniqueness is incomparable. You are born with royalty, you are a child of destiny, you are created to impact your territory positively and pass it on to the generation after you. You are loaded with heavenly treasures that are meant to utilize on earth. You are the light the world has been waiting for to shine in the darkness. You are the one to deliver those who are yet to identify their identity. You are the hope of many generations. You are here at this time for this reason. You are full of extensive endowments that can only be measured by God. Therefore, believe and value the greatness that God has deposited in you. It is given to you to discover You, your purpose, and manifest. Discovering your uniqueness is discovering your world.

More so, if you understand the magnitude of your identity as an individual, you will be able to operate in the reality of the power in you. What makes you different from others is the supernatural power that you carry. The scripture says in Romans 8: 19, "For the earnest expectation of the creation eagerly waits for the revealing of the sons of God". This means that you have a unique potential that only you can offer to the world. Individuals, people, and nations are waiting for you to manifest. There are numerous problems people are facing, that only the power bestowed on you by God can solve. A lot of people are in bondage waiting for you to deliver them. Many are in the wilderness of life crying for help, some are suffering from poverty. A lot of people are dying of hunger, no food to eat. Health crisis is alarming, people are passing away because of sickness. This is the time to set this generation free from unpleasant situation. You are born to save a life. You have been chosen to bring restoration to the people who are still struggling to identify themselves. This is the time to use the power invested in you at work because you have a time limit on earth. It is a wonderful thing to know who you are and recognize the power you carry, and it is more glorious to make use of it. Life makes really sense when you know your identity and utilize it. Understanding oneself is understanding God's power in YOU!

CHAPTER THREE
Steps to Success

The purpose of existence is to know the reason why you are created and accomplish it. The journey of life is like climbing a ladder. Each ladder has its own obstacles, challenges, and breakthroughs. It is very paramount to identify your purpose in life. If you knew what you were called to do, you would succeed irrespective of the stumbling blocks on your way to climbing ladders of greatness in life. According to google, it describes "Ladder as a structure consisting of series of bars or steps between two upright lengths of wood, or rope, used for climbing up or down something" It means that there are many steps to climbing before getting to the zenith of a ladder. If you want to achieve a goal that you set for yourself, you have to take a step forward with the aim of attaining the goal. There are different types of ladders, and they have limited durations. Every Ladder is composed of steps and each step climbed takes you to the next one. A quick question is that, what do you project ahead of you?

Moreover, everyone has a specific ladder divinely made for them. This means that God gives you a special gift that is uniquely crafted for you. Therefore, all you need to do, is to identify your special ladder and walk on the steps to achieving your purpose. Your ladder is meant for you, nobody can walk through it better than you. Everything you need to accomplish your goals has been provided for you on your ladder, so focus on it. You are required to focus and pay attention to the things that happen in your space. There are things that will appear as distractions to distract you from moving forward. Do not get distracted while climbing the stairs up to avoid falling. Do not be preoccupied with nothing on each stair, ensure you are occupied with relevant assignment. Do not compare your ladder to others because yours is different. Nobody can run your race and achieve your goal better than you. You have to face the reality that your ladder is originally made for you alone. Often times, some people tend to walk on other people's ladders forgetting theirs. Some imitate others out of ignorant, and others try to follow the trend. This is a very dangerous mistake, because they will struggle through each step and will never get to achieve their purpose in life. The scripture made it clear in Romans 12:6-8, that God gave everyone a special gift according to their abilities to use it on earth to glorify Him and share the testimonies to others to be blessed. God is perfect in all His ways. He gives everyone He created with gifts perfectly designed for them. Every gift you have is designed for you, you are the only one that can use the gift perfectly. When God gives you a talent, He provides all the necessary equipment needed to back it up. He does not deposit great virtues into your life for nothing. He has a reason for every gift He gives.

Furthermore, every step in a ladder represents realities of life. Each step is different from the other. The first two steps may be easy to climb, while the next one may seem difficult for you. It depends on how your ladder is being orchestrated. This does not mean that one will not arrive at the final destination. You cannot predict it until you take a walk on it. While journey through the steps, you may experience setbacks, disappointments, failures, hardship and success, do not give up on your journey to the utmost ladder. These are part of your package to the top, be positive to yourself and everyone around you, guard your thoughts not to have control over you and beware of friends that may see you as unserious fellow, because they are not in the same ladder with you. They may seem not to understand the purpose, it is okay. The good news is that, when you climb a step and overcome its obstacle, it leads you to a greater level in life, at the moment when you see yourself overcoming challenges that are meant to stop you, take a break, sit down, and reflect on how you overcame and thank God for the victory. Then, pat yourself at the back and keep your head high. Keep striving for excellence, do not limit yourself. Always put your confidence in God and never forget that He is always with you to help you through the challenges and storms of life. Remember that your condition does not limit the presence of God in your life. Return all glory to the owner of your life and share your testimonies with family and friends of how God help you to succeed.

CHAPTER FOUR
Endurance

The ability to endure the test of time without compromising is a great characteristic. In other words, Endurance is one of the gifts of the Holy spirit that God empowered into everyone. You need to activate it to be able to get familiar with it. To ensure your success in life, you have to be patience with yourself and others. Life is full surprises, sometimes what you plan is not what you always get but at the end of it all, it makes sense. Life is challenging and interesting at the same time. So, be patience and expectant of the things that will happen in your life, it could be greater than what you ever planned for. I remembered a couple of years ago, when I gave birth to my girls (triplets), I had to stay in the hospital for two Months because of some complications as a result of the birth. I was going through unbearable pains all over my body. I could not eat nor sleep for seven days. However, as days go by, my faith grew stronger in the Lord. I encouraged myself with the word of God that says my grace is sufficient for you, for my power is made perfect in weakness.

More so, I knew that God was with me, because He puts His Angels in my life and saw me through the pregnancy, I knew He would not abandon me, He has brought me to the end of the pregnancy so He cannot forsake me at the moment. His grace was my sufficiency so I relayed on His unfailing words. His word is life that delivers His people. His word was the food I ate throughout the period of the pain. His word keeps assuring me that the storm would soon be over, I strongly believed in the word of God. I endured the pain with smile on my face each day. My family and friends could not understand the smile on my face because some of them knew what I was going through but wondering why I smile. I was the one reassuring them that all would be alright, despite my pain. I was able to convince them that God brought me into it and would take me out of the storm. After seven days of pain, God took away my sorrow and gloriously restored everything my health. I have trusted Him all my life and He had never failed me. Patience is an attribute that attracts the supernatural power of God into your life, it is the power that controls your mind. When you embrace patience, you allow the spirit of God to direct you to His purpose for your life.

In this age of technology, where everything is digital, many people want to get what they supposed to get in twenty years, right now. Some think that the way things are working more faster that is how their life should be, not knowing that life is a stage and each stage has a requirement to be met before exceeding to the next stage. Patience is the key to success, every step you take is attached with challenges and victories. There is no an examination without a test. The period of testing, is a period of endurance. Once you passed the examination, you are automatically promoted to the next level. While preparing for the test, you study, take notes, reassess yourself; you are exercising patience in the process. Unconsciously, some people do practice endurance without knowing it. The application of patience during a challenging time helps a person in building internal stability. Sometimes it can be difficult to endure hardship but with the grace of God, you will overcome. The one who created you has endowed you with everything you need as an individual to endure. Everyone has the gift of endurance inside of them. The problem with some people is that, they are not conscious of who they are and what they have. You must know who you are created to be, what you represent, and where you are going, to ensure you accomplish your purpose.

Knowing who you are is knowing the God who made you. Endurance is the key of life.

ACTIVATION PRAYERS

Proverbs 19:21, Many are the plans in a person's heart, but it is the Lord's purpose that prevails.

1. *Thank You Lord, for Your plans for my life.*

2. *I know that your desire for my life is better than what I can imagine*

3. *I acknowledge your everlasting generosity in my family*

4. *Lord, lead me to the paths of your righteousness, so I can fulfill my purpose in life.*

5. *Heavenly father, help me to know who you created me to be, so I can save my generation.*

6. *Oh Lord, give me the grace to identify my divine purpose, so I will use it to glorify your Name on earth.*

7. *Lord, grant me the grace to endure every challenge of life in order to achieve my divine purpose.*

8. *Oh Lord, give me the grace to identify my destiny helper this season.*

9. *Lord, You are my Original DESTINY HELPER, connect me to my helpers.*

10. *Father, bless and keep my destiny helpers in Jesus's name. Amen*